TIME TO BUY YOUR PERFECT HOME

A simple guide for the first-time property buyers in Dubai

Anastasia Dorokhina

Time to Buy Your Perfect Home
Copyright © 2021 Anastasia Dorokhina
First published in 2021

ISBN
Print: 978-1-922456-26-7
E-book: 978-1-922456-27-4

All rights reserved. No part of this book may be reproduced, stored in a retrieval system, or transmitted by any means (electronic, mechanical, photocopying, recording, or otherwise) without written permission from the author.

Because of the dynamic nature of the Internet, any web addresses or links contained in this book may have changed since publication and may no longer be valid. The information in this book is based on the author's experiences and opinions. The views expressed in this book are solely those of the author and do not necessarily reflect the views of the publisher; the publisher hereby disclaims any responsibility for them.

The author of this book does not dispense any form of medical, legal, financial, or technical advice either directly or indirectly. The intent of the author is solely to provide information of a general nature to help you in your quest for personal development and growth. In the event you use any of the information in this book, the author and the publisher assume no responsibility for your actions. If any form of expert assistance is required, the services of a competent professional should be sought.

Publishing information
Publishing, design, and production facilitated by Passionpreneur Publishing, A division of Passionpreneur Organization Pty Ltd, ABN: 48640637529

www.PassionpreneurPublishing.com
Melbourne, VIC | Australia

TABLE OF CONTENTS

My Dubai Story	1
House Versus Home	9
What Are You Buying: Property or Lifestyle?	21
How to Find a Project That Excites You	35
Every Home Buyer's Dream	45
The Psychology of Buying a Home	53
Dubai: Holiday Destination, Investment, or Home?	67
How Do You Finance Your Property?	75
Common Mistakes to Avoid	83
Conclusion	91
About the Author	95

MY DUBAI STORY

Home is not a place . . . it's a feeling.

"Anastasia, why don't you try your hand at real estate? You have what it takes!" said my leasing agent as we were signing the documents for my new rental contract.

"Are you kidding, Aboubakar? There is absolutely no way I am going to have this hectic lifestyle of a real estate agent! Thank you for considering me though," I responded, while putting my initials on the pages.

We became good friends with this brilliant agent, who worked really hard and was very patient with me, showing me multiple units and negotiating a really good deal for me. We laughed over his "proposal" of me becoming a real estate agent, and ever since, we have constantly been in touch.

A few months down the line, I realised that I have been in Dubai for six years; the time went by so fast, and it felt like only a couple of years. Being an expat in Dubai, I always thought of short-term plans, whether it was renewing my rent or job contract for another term. At that moment, I realised that short-term planning through the six years had cost me a lot of money on rent and that I should rather start exploring the option of investing in my own asset, in my own property, in Dubai.

And thus, my real estate journey began. But I didn't know where to start my research, as there was no one in my network who could advise me properly, except my leasing agent Aboubakar.

However, I needed leverage and expert advice in many aspects. The first thing that most people do in this situation is to go to the property portal and start looking at different listings. So, this is where I started as well. I consumed a lot of information, checking listing after listing, discovering some of Dubai's districts that I had never even heard about. I checked photos, did Google research, and—to summarise it all—I just drowned in this overwhelming amount of information.

While I was browsing portals, I also saw information on mortgage provided, property prices, and market performance. That was quite a lot to take into consideration from the start. I was confused and had many questions. I was in a dilemma whether to buy a ready property or something under construction. How was I to finance it? How would I choose the right property that will appreciate with time? What's the amount of down payment?

I shortlisted options and called on ads, but the listing agents were not very keen to understand what I actually needed advice on; rather, they tried to offer and push for what they had. I talked to some of my friends who had recently bought properties; it turned out that they had been through the same experience and shared the same disappointments I did. I realised that I didn't know much about Dubai communities as I would drive to work from Dubai World Trade Centre to DIFC and hang out at Palm Jumeirah/Marina area, and I had no clue that there was life beyond Sheikh Zayed Road.

To get a better understanding of the process—financing, legal aspects, and market performance—I looked for further information on blogs and portals, reading articles on expat communities' websites. I got more confused as the information I found was either contradictory, outdated, or too light and generic to give me proper insights for my action plan.

I also talked to salespeople, but they confused me even more because either they were not professionals or they went into too many technical details that I just didn't understand at all.

On asking advice from my friends, I got even more confused, as they gave me references of their real estate agents, who could not advise me clearly at the initial search stage. It seemed like they were only ready to work with buyers who would finalise on the spot. I kept getting more confused and coming back to square one.

I started reading news about the real estate market regularly, and as a result, I began to actually question whether I needed to buy a property in Dubai, considering all the negativity about the market that I discovered in some of the news.

To go deeper, I started reading reports on the website of Dubai Land Department, hoping to receive precise information from the right source; however, I was frustrated again with the technical language and trying to interpret the numbers, which didn't make any sense to me.

While there were multiple resources and analytics to dig into, it required a lot of time to go through this content, since I am not a big fan of crunching numbers on Excel sheets, neither do I enjoy reading boring laws and legislations. The content targeted professionals, analysts, and experienced investors but not first-time home buyers. I realised that there was no comprehensive, easy-to-follow system on how to find and choose a perfect home for first-time home buyers in Dubai. So I collected bits and pieces and insights of useful information and advice that were actually valuable and put them all together in my notes.

After a couple of months of research and viewings, I developed an understanding of what my home in Dubai should be, how I would feel living there, and how it will serve and complement my lifestyle; most importantly, I got to know how to turn my dream home from thoughts into reality and finalise a down payment.

"Home is not a place, it's a feeling." I realised that the feeling associated with my home began with feelings about the community and location of my home. I asked myself in which community I wanted to live. How do I feel about different communities in Dubai? The choice was between urban-city vibes, serene and quiet green golf course communities, and popular waterfront urban districts. I wanted to have a bit of everything in the community where I was going to live—isolated in peace and tranquillity and at the same time in the middle of action, with a possibility of choosing the mode, whenever I wanted, depending on the mood. Yet the community had to be centrally positioned within the city, easily accessible to major landmarks and districts, making it easy for me to drive around this busy city without getting stuck in traffic. I discovered that I appreciate modern design, so my perfect home had to have floor-to-ceiling windows, with a lot of daylight and lovely views.

I also realised that by the end of my research, after consuming so much information, I had actually become quite aware of the communities, projects, market, and real estate transactions in Dubai. This got me thinking, why don't I actually become one of the real estate agents? Now that I had experienced the customer journey and seen the gaps, I could actually fill them in by bringing my knowledge and passion and add value. That was another of my aha moments, where I decided to switch from my corporate career to real estate brokerage.

Joining the real estate agency and becoming an industry expert resulted in taking my home search to another level. I got to know much more about the business and transactions from inside out, and new opportunities opened up.

I sincerely enjoyed my journey that started from a home search and resulted in my becoming a real estate agent; however, I wish there was somebody for me right in the beginning who was genuinely interested and qualified, yet empathetic, to help me in this journey from A to Z to find me a perfect home.

I have always liked to help and bring value to people who need any advice, based on my own experience and lessons learned. It makes me feel good when I help people and I see them happy and thankful. No money can buy this feeling of being helpful and bringing value to people.

I have come to realise that there gaps in the industry and some kind of lost connections among first-time home buyers, sellers, and other market counterparties. I wanted to contribute positively in creating a synergy between all of them by providing knowledge to the first-time home buyers and explaining to the counterparties the challenges that people go through during their journey of finding their perfect home.

I saw room for improvement and wanted to make a positive contribution by sharing my experience.

Throughout my career, I held positions within business development and marketing across real estate, investment, financial services, and management consulting industries. I have an MBA in International Business Management from a US-based university. My expat life started years before coming to Dubai—in the US back in 2009, where I have experienced different cultures and traditions through communicating with different nationalities. This experience helped me to understand their values and requirements better, when it comes to choosing a home and lifestyle.

Later, when I moved to Dubai, I managed investor relations, business development, and marketing for a US$5 billion asset management company. While I was approaching the largest investment institutions and investment corporations in GCC and in the world with our company's investment proposals, I learned that the majority of investors preferred allocating the biggest chunks of their investment to real estate assets. Hence, I feel very confident—thanks to my experience of interacting with large corporate investors worldwide—that investment in a property is the safest and most appreciated investment one can have.

During my research on the property market in Dubai, I have studied and analysed reports and data by the largest consulting firms, local reports by UAE's market counterparties, records of Dubai Land Department, and law and regulations, and gained insights from the world's top real estate investors and speakers at the real estate conferences and events.

Throughout my experience of finding perfect homes for my clients, I have managed inquiries from small apartments to exclusive mansions and have dealt with budgets of all sizes and complex requirements, regardless of language barriers and time zone differences.

What's important is that for my international clients, I was their first Dubai ambassador, lifestyle concierge, or legal and financial advisor. This was way before we were actually moving to sourcing and arranging properties for them, as they required a lot of groundwork to be done for them before they could make a decision to choose Dubai as a destination for their home.

I decided to create a guide for first-time home buyers in Dubai who were struggling to find their perfect home for various reasons—whether they didn't have the time or patience to look at many options—as they wanted to have an absolutely stress-free experience. Therefore, they needed well-structured advice, based on deep market research, catering to their specific criteria, which would enable them to make a quick decision on making a safe investment in their first home and thereby enjoy their life in Dubai.

However, there were also cases where people were stretching their research for months without making a decision because they were left to do their research on their own, and this was leading them nowhere as their confusion and frustration only increased.

I came up with an easy-to-follow system to identify, shortlist, and choose the right property to educate first-time property buyers about all they need to know to find and secure their perfect home.

I realised that one of the best ways to help people, regardless of whether they are planning to buy properties in Dubai or not, is to share the knowledge that I have accumulated. Therefore, I have summarised my experience and research in the next chapters of this book to help and guide thousands of people whom I can't physically or remotely work with on finding their perfect home owing to the time limitations we all have.

HOUSE VERSUS HOME

*A house is made with walls and beams;
a home is built with love and dreams.*

—Ralph Waldo Emerson

A home is something that represents our entire world. Home is where we feel safe . . . a place we love, we learn, we work, and we overcome challenges. Home is a place that will always be there to protect us. Home is where we connect with what we treasure the most. Home is where our dreams are made and beautiful memories are created. These are intangible emotional assets that we will carry all through our lives in our hearts.

What is a house then? It is a property, an asset, that we look at from a purely investment point of view. We evaluate it based on its value for money, market value, return on investment, price per sq. ft., and many other criteria.

When most Dubai expats start thinking about buying a property after spending years in Dubai, their main motivation is to stop burning money on rent. As I was researching on the subject for myself, I realised that my first residence would be the underlying cornerstone asset to grow financially. So eventually, I had to find a property that would represent a hybrid of house and home to achieve both of my goals. My first home was supposed to become a long-term investment—both emotionally and financially—and making such an investment requires a framework, which I will be sharing with you in this chapter.

Let me ask you a question: Do you want to live in a nice home and enjoy a good lifestyle with your family? And perhaps you want another property or more than one property as an income-generating asset to pay for your lifestyle?

I guess your answer is "Yes."

Now, let me ask you another question: Why don't you have one yet? Assuming that you are reading my book, I presume you already have an interest in real estate in Dubai. However, something is stopping you from actually embarking on the journey of finding and owning Your Perfect Home.

While you are searching for your answer, I am going to bring to your attention the top four misconceptions about owning your own home in Dubai, and perhaps at least one of them will resonate with you. Here they are:

- Thinking of buying a house at some point in the future, when actually your future is made of decisions you make today.

- You should only buy a property when you are in your thirties, forties, or when you are financially stable.
- Females think that they should start thinking about investing in real estate after getting married as a joint purchase with the spouse, or they assume that their spouses will be dealing with the process of finding and financing the property, and they will only get involved into the process when it comes to choosing the curtains and furniture.
- Thinking that buying a property in Dubai is expensive, impossible, difficult . . . you name it!

Before we dig deeper, let's take a look at this graph to determine whether you are ready to take one of the most important financial and emotional decisions in your life—to buy a house.

My sincere congratulations if you have chosen to start your journey of *Time to Buy Your Perfect Home*. This book will be really helpful for you throughout the journey. However, if you haven't arrived there during this exercise, do not put this book aside yet. You can still learn many tips as you progress, and by the time you are financially and emotionally ready for a new home, you would already be familiar with everything you need to know to move straight to searching for your dream house.

"I will forever believe that buying a home is a great investment. Why? Because you can't live in a stock certificate. You can't live in a mutual fund," said Oprah Winfrey, who is not only a media mogul, a philanthropist, and an actress, but also happens to be a real estate tycoon.

TIME TO BUY YOUR PERFECT HOME

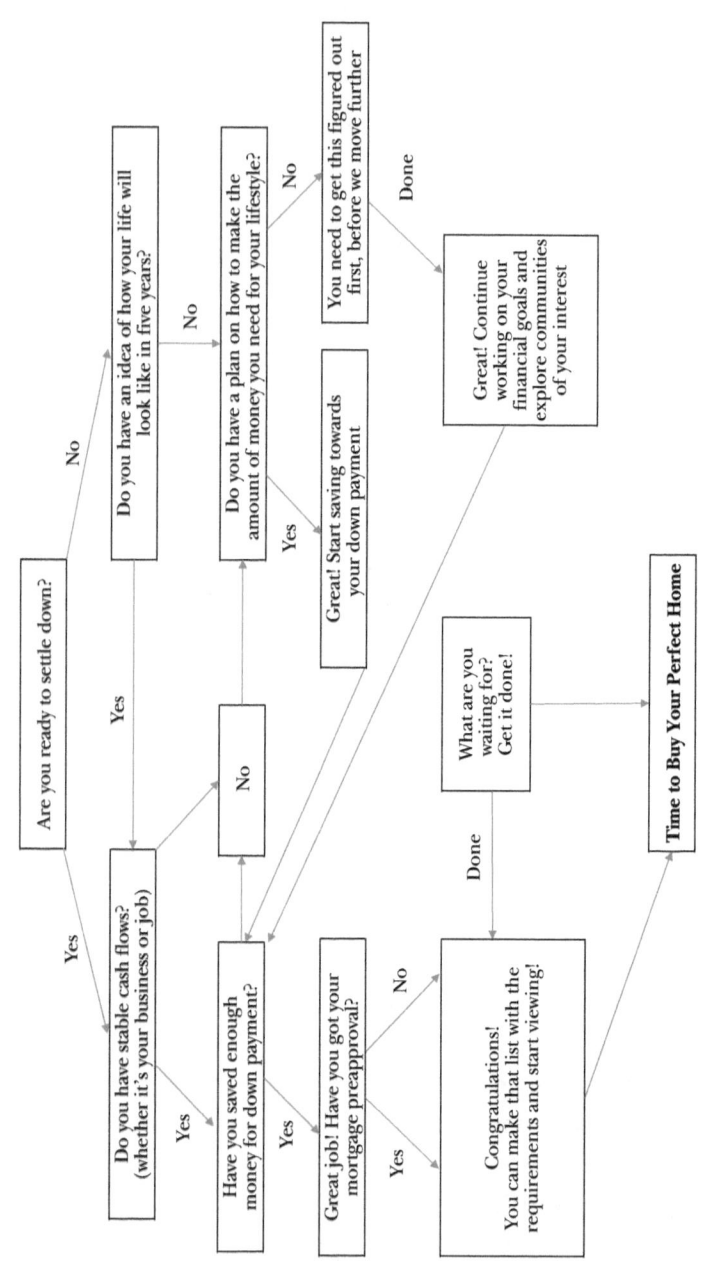

With all due respect to other investment-asset classes, I believe that the most natural, logical, and safest way to build wealth is to start by investing first in your own residential property. Let's go through the breakdown of "WHYs":

- Property is a good source of a long-term passive or secondary income and it creates generational wealth.
- It pays for itself, its maintenance cost, and other expenses when it's rented out.
- Unlike stock markets, its value doesn't fluctuate due to various events (pandemics, political disturbances, etc.).
- It can be re-mortgaged or used as a collateral to finance your other assets.
- It generates capital appreciation over the years.
- Residential property is the only asset class that can be utilised for personal use—it can be your home!

Therefore, buying a property should be looked at as buying a home to live in and, at the same time, as acquisition of a quality investment asset for a more affluent future. What is also worth noting is that there is no specific, perfect time to buy a home; in general, earlier is better.

"Ninety per cent of all millionaires become so through owning real estate. More money has been made in real estate than in all industrial investments combined. The wise young man or wage earner of today invests his money in real estate," said Andrew Carnegie, billionaire industrialist.

It's proven that investing in real estate on a long-term basis generates wealth, so the earlier you start, the better it is. I personally regret that I didn't plan on buying a property much earlier. If I had thought of buying a property when I received my first paycheque, it would have had a great impact on my life in so many different ways—financial, professional, and personal. I wish someone could have explained this to me before or led me by their example of generating wealth by investing in real estate. I am glad though that now so much information is available and accessible online so that people can actually access and use it.

So who are those people who made significant wealth in real estate?

In one of her interviews with *The National newspaper*, Donna Benton, the founder of the Entertainer, the two-for-one UAE dining, beauty, and leisure deals company, shared that she invests a lot in property. "It's an automatic saving," she says. "If you go broke you've got somewhere to live. Property appreciates; it's a guaranteed return." Donna invests in holiday homes, where she would like to travel, but she also rents them out and gets a return. As per Donna, her best property investment in Dubai was a one-bedroom apartment in JLT, bought off-plan fifteen years ago, where at some point she was getting a 20 per cent return.

Let's also look at some examples of individuals in other countries who made their wealth in real estate.

Barbara Corcoran is an American businesswoman and the founder of the Corcoran Group, New York's premier real estate brokerage. She made her wealth in real estate by starting small.

"I bought my first itty-bitty studio after scraping together a few bucks because I needed to live somewhere anyway. A few years later, the studio doubled in value, giving me enough cash to plunk down 50 per cent on a one-bedroom apartment. That soon rolled into a two-bedroom, then a three-bedroom, and finally landed me in my 10-room penthouse on Fifth Avenue in New York City. Buying that tiny studio was the most important decision I made because it got me in the game."

That's absolutely true. Homes come in every size and budget. Your first property doesn't have to be an expensive mansion. Not knowing about affordable projects and ways of financing properties lead many people to continue renting, making it costlier for themselves as they are burning their money on rent for years.

Many women think that independence and the ability to have their own funds are very important in life. But financial stability and wealth come not only from having a job that pays the bills but also from investing in their own real estate assets. In an article in *Gulf News* in 2018, it mentions that according to statistics by the Dubai Land Department, around 30 per cent of Dubai's property is owned by women. Think about it—three out of ten properties in Dubai are owned by women. This shows the accumulation of large amounts of wealth in female hands.

To make things smooth and easy in your home-buying process, you should have a clear understanding of four major areas of your journey, which I have grouped into sections for your easy reference.

1. Emotions
    a. **What kind of lifestyle are you living?**
    First of all, what does a "lifestyle" mean? In general, lifestyle refers to a combination of anything that we repeatedly do—work, behaviour, leisure, and social patterns. It affects our identity and how we see ourselves. When it comes to lifestyle property, we refer to leisure, physical health, and emotional well-being. In other words, lifestyle property represents an added value to our quality of life. It's important to look at your daily habits honestly and determine what your little joys are at home.

    Your dream home should be a reflection of who you are. Deciding on the location is just the starting point of your journey. You will also need to decide on your expectations and the life you want to live in order to find the home that will be just right for you.

    In the chapter dedicated to the lifestyle, I give concrete examples of real people and explain why it is important to consider the lifestyle component when it comes to choosing a property and what impact this decision has on your quality of life.
    b. **The psychology of buying a home:**
    How do our emotions affect the decision-making process? There is no doubt that buying or selling a home is among the most stressful events in people's lives. In order to make sure that you don't get blinded by your emotions under stress during such an important process, I will be sharing practical tips on how to segregate emotional and rational factors in your decision-making process. I will also share two different

approaches in the home-buying process by males and females. That will be an interesting read, especially if you are buying a house as a couple. You will need to deal with different points of view and come up with a mutually agreeable decision.

2. Process
   a. **How do you find an exciting project?**
   Dubai is one of the most beautiful and dynamic cities in the world. The first emotion that comes to my memory during my first visit to Dubai is excitement going through the roof. Everything is so exciting here that I never stop being charmed even after six years of living here. Breaking the Guinness World Records one after another, Dubai is known as the unstoppable city with no limits. The tallest buildings, the largest manmade islands, the largest crystal lagoon in the world . . . the list goes on and on.

   What is really interesting is that absolutely each community and each project in Dubai has its own specific flavour—the really exciting feature that defines it. For Downtown it's Burj Khalifa, for District 1 it's the Crystal Lagoon, for Dubai Marina it's the canal with promenades, and Palm Jumeirah speaks for itself.

   Each newly launched project appears to be more exciting than the previous one. With so many different options, how do we choose where to live and not miss out on the really exciting community? The chapter about finding an exciting project that is right for you provides you with step-by-step guidance on identifying your needs through a series of questions and analysing the outcome.

b. **How do you identify and actually choose the right property?**

There are three major types of residential properties in each community in Dubai—apartments, townhouses, and villas—all based on different parameters with their own pros and cons that are determined individually for every home owner. It's important to understand the advantages and disadvantages that matter to you before making a decision, and you'll also have to weigh your needs. I will be sharing an easy-to-follow methodology to identify which property type suits you best, if you haven't determined it as yet. As a bonus, you will be given a few tips on how to pick the best unit in the project.

3. Numbers
   a. **How do you finance your house?**

   There are many different ways of financing your property in Dubai. In most cases, your decision on the financing terms will be tied up closely to the type of property that you are choosing. For example, if you are selecting an off-plan property, you have an option to go with the payment plan from the developer. In case you are going for a ready property, in most cases, you would consider mortgage financing with the bank. There are also cases when you are considering an off-plan property, but you can still benefit from the payment plan during construction, and then you have an option to mortgage it on completion. Then there is when you are going for a ready property with a payment plan. In this chapter, you will learn how to choose the right financing method that suits you the best.

b. **Holiday homes as a lucrative investment opportunity**
Dubai offers significantly higher property rental returns when compared to London, New York, Hong Kong, and Singapore. And ever since holiday homes' legal framework was introduced in Dubai in 2016, the industry has been booming, with more and more homes coming on the market each day. Besides enjoying your vacation in Dubai at your holiday home, you can see good returns on your property by renting it out for short-term use the rest of the year. In this chapter, I walk you through a methodology of choosing the right holiday home and share the latest trends on Dubai's holiday home market.

4. Pitfalls
There are quite a lot of mistakes first-time home buyers make, and I cover the most common ones in the chapter dedicated to mistakes. However, to give you a heads-up before you get to that very last chapter of the book, you should be mindful of these top three mistakes:

a. Not knowing your financials and budget.
b. Conducting inadequate research on the locality and prices.
c. Making rushed or emotional decisions.

This book will be your go-to manual for making the right decision when it is *Time To Buy Your Perfect Home*. As long as you follow the chapters in this book, you will feel that this journey is pleasant and interesting, as you move to your final destination at Your Perfect Home.

Buying a house can be the best thing you've ever done—or the worst. This book will guide you throughout the journey and will supply you with the right advice.

I am very excited to take you on this journey of finding your perfect home in Dubai and helping you to fill in the blanks of knowledge and information that you need in order to make one of the most important decisions in your life.

WHAT ARE YOU BUYING: PROPERTY OR LIFESTYLE?

I've met many people in Dubai who have relocated here from other countries, and at the very beginning of their search for properties, they were very specific about the type of lifestyle property they were looking for. This was because they were primarily looking for a community that would offer them the same lifestyle they had in their home country before relocating to Dubai.

They would do extensive online research on various options and would ask their colleagues, friends, and real estate agents to send them live videos and overviews about the properties and communities of their interest to shortlist a few options. I've seen people who were precisely matching their "virtual" expectations with the realities of their dream Dubai lifestyle, and, at the same time, I saw people who were actually taking 180-degree reverse turns on their requirements and reconsidering the entire house-hunting process after arriving in Dubai.

Another category is those who had to actually find themselves here and chose how they want to live and where. For some of them, it was very obvious what kind of lifestyle they would prefer. For example, a majority of the people from "cold" Russia and CIS countries would choose to live by the beach, while others who are actually exposed to warm climate and beaches would be looking for completely different communities—city districts like Downtown or Dubai Marina or golf course communities. In this chapter, you will get more familiar with the lifestyles that Dubai has to offer, and you will also receive guidance on how to choose your lifestyle, if you haven't discovered yet what suits you the most.

Your first step would be to understand which is a better fit for you—a house or a lifestyle property.

What is a lifestyle property?
Lifestyle property is a phrase that you've perhaps heard lately. But what does it actually mean? A lifestyle property is a home that has one or more unique features that help improve the daily quality of life. Though a house and a lifestyle property each provide a dwelling in which to live, a lifestyle property offers something extra that a house does not. To live a healthy lifestyle, your home has to offer a healthy environment—it shouldn't drain you. Home is where you spend most of your time, and therefore it must support your physical health and your emotional well-being.

Let me just give you a few examples of lifestyle properties so that you get a better idea:

- Waterfront and beachfront properties
- Private island properties
- Golf course properties

- Lakeside properties
- Historic properties

Choosing the right neighbourhood and location of the property based on lifestyle is one of the most important decisions a person makes in their adult life, because a house is not only a significant financial investment but also a health investment. The right house for you is the house that best meets your unique needs and is within the parameters of your budget.

For example, if you are a golfer or a gardener, would you enjoy or feel satisfied living in a busy city district with high-rise buildings and no greenery around? If you were born in the city with the beachfront next to your doorstep, would you choose to live in a golf course community or urban city district? To a great extent, our lifestyle and preferences determine the type of community we choose to live in. By the end of this chapter, you will learn how to identify the best suitable community and property that matches and complements your lifestyle.

Dubai lifestyles
Think about it, why are you living in Dubai? Is it because you moved and stayed here for your new job? Is it because of opportunities for doing business? Or maybe because you like the variety of lifestyle choices that Dubai offers? In Dubai, you can start your day with a morning dip at the beach, go for a nice afternoon golf game, and then enjoy the throbbing nightlife in Downtown or Marina.

Do you want to know why I live here? I absolutely love Dubai for its unstoppable development, its ambitions, and the opportunities that it offers to all its residents. Dubai has become a city of the future, offering its residents and guests different lifestyles to enjoy. The issue of finding the right lifestyle in Dubai that you feel comfortable with is as confusing as walking into the biggest Friday brunch and not knowing what to choose. Whatever kind of lifestyle you are looking for, you are still spoiled for choices, and hence it's really confusing.

One of my friends recently revealed to me a story about his journey of changing his lifestyle in Dubai. We were sitting on the beach in the evening, listening to the sound of the waves in "his beach garden" and burning firewood, as he told his story.

He had been living abroad for many years and has been in Dubai for four years. He found that actually there is no perfect place on earth and concluded, based on his personal experience, that for a good life "you have to have a good base where you live and at the same time, travel as often as you can." And he found that Dubai has it all—a variety of lifestyle choices and a perfect, strategic location, allowing residents and tourists to travel almost anywhere in the world, with the average duration of a flight being eight hours. I remember him saying, "Overall, Dubai wins somehow."

After spending over four years in DIFC, living in a high-rise building in a busy business district with a bustling nightlife with bars and restaurants, and heavy traffic in rush hours, one day he asked himself a question: "What am I doing here? Am I missing something?" Shortly after asking himself this question, he realised that he actually wanted to explore a seaside community with a peaceful and relaxing environment, where

WHAT ARE YOU BUYING: PROPERTY OR LIFESTYLE?

each detail would contribute to making him feel good. He wanted this change for a healthier lifestyle with some different vibes. For him, quality of life was a very important requirement, something that he didn't want to compromise on. He also wanted to share a beautiful outdoor space that he would enjoy with friends, but without having a villa. He also wanted to have a unique setup and environment that his friends would find attractive so they would come and visit him. He gave me an example—that everyone has a pool in their building, and you cannot surprise anyone with this kind of amenity in Dubai. Furthermore, he wanted to be at someplace where he would feel like he is going out, without actually having a need to go out and drive anywhere.

So he started his search for a perfect place that would offer him the lifestyle change that he was craving for. He explored the most popular waterfront communities in Dubai. However, despite their appeal, he was not 100 per cent convinced about them and could not figure out what was missing there. Viewing after viewing, he was getting frustrated, as his expectations didn't match with the opportunities that were available. Later he realised what the missing piece of the puzzle was about all those waterfront communities that he had visited—he never heard the sound of the waves there. He realised that not only did he want to enjoy the beautiful waterfront views, but he also wanted to experience the sea and nature through the sound of the waves, which would make him calm down when he returned home from work every day.

Fortunately, he found his dream home. It is located directly on a beautiful beach with natural waves that, in windy weather, make this sound that makes his soul happy. He was happy to find a compromise for a large outdoor space, where he can invite his friends, without having a villa. He felt totally different vibes while spending his first week at the new home, and noticed that his sleep became deeper and more relaxed. In just a matter of a few days, he already got to know the majority of his neighbours, who hung out at the "beach garden," just like him, enjoying the peace and tranquillity of the seaside.

When I first started to think about finding my perfect home, I was really confused about the lifestyle and community I desired. Furthermore, I was not sure if I could afford the premium price that lifestyle properties come with, as I clearly saw the difference in the way those lifestyle properties are priced. Being very adventurous and curious about different experiences and activities, such as biking, paddle boarding, and other water sports, I really could not understand and prioritise my preferred options on what would be my perfect community in Dubai. As my routines and hobbies are constantly changing and evolving, I didn't want to limit myself to one set of amenities in my neighbourhood.

So I just started exploring communities, visiting new places, and spending more time in places that I considered I could live in. Otherwise, how would you know that you like something if you have never tried it? We are all familiar with the bustling cosmopolitan lifestyle of Downtown and Dubai Marina, which are Dubai's most popular areas. However, have you ever been to the new developments like Dubai Creek, District 1, or Dubai Hills, for example? So, if you haven't yet been there, it's time to explore!

WHAT ARE YOU BUYING: PROPERTY OR LIFESTYLE?

One of my friends recently told me that he just fell in love with one particular community when he tried a cycling track there. The feeling of joy from this experience was so strong for him that he became enthusiastic about checking options for apartments and villas for sale in that community. I realised that the best way of finding out where you will feel more comfortable is by actually:

- Going and experiencing hobbies, activities, and places.
- Closing your eyes and fast-forwarding a few years into the future and imagining whom you are with and what you are doing. For example, for me, my first property was supposed to be my first asset. I was thinking of turning it into an investment after living there for a couple of years. Therefore, when I was making a choice, I was thinking that it should reflect my lifestyle and me for the next two to three years. However, if you already have family and kids and are looking to move from a rental property into your own home, you will have a different set of criteria and checklists to consider.
- Have you ever gone window-shopping for clothing? We've all been there, right? When you are just taking a look, knowing very well that you won't be taking out your credit card. Well, window-shopping for a property is just as common. Attend that open house event in the community that you haven't been to but have heard nice reviews about from your friends and colleagues; stop by at the café to have lunch in that community on the way from the open house. Go and explore, without any intention to buy, and see how you feel about different properties. I know that many real

estate sales agents will hate me for this, but I care more about helping you find a perfect home, not about sales agents. Seeing multiple houses and apartments before making a decision serves numerous purposes. It gives you something to measure up against, and we all need benchmarks.

Exploring the amenities
What makes your lifestyle property sophisticated and perfect for you is, in fact, a good match between location and amenities that are right for you. When reviewing potential properties, you should pay great attention to amenities, both within the residence and those surrounding it. For example, if you and your family enjoy frequent boat trips and "seacation" weekends, do you require your beachfront property to have a yacht club or marina nearby for convenient and smooth logistics around boat trips? Is it important for you that the gym in the residence will be in the building on podium level or on the highest level with magnificent panoramic views of the Dubai skyline? Do you want to do your morning swimming laps in the largest and highest building in the city in an infinity swimming pool? Or you actually prefer to do your laps in the sea? You need to decide which elements are most important and which will give you the comfort you deserve, as only *you* know the vital details that will impact your life the most.

Similar to key neighbourhoods in London, Paris, and New York, there are some areas in Dubai that will never go out of fashion, that rise above the standards, and are on everyone's dream list. These are Downtown, Palm Jumeirah, and Emirates Hills, to name just a few.

WHAT ARE YOU BUYING: PROPERTY OR LIFESTYLE?

The residents of Downtown would typically enjoy living in this district because of the feeling of being at the beating heart of the city, as there is so much to do and see—enjoying amazing views of Burj Khalifa, exploring fine dining at the best restaurants in five-star hotels, seeing amazing performances at Dubai Opera, and meeting all types of people from different places around the world. It's also very convenient for getting around the city, being a short drive to DIFC, Dubai World Trade Centre, the beach, and the airport.

People who live for a long time at the Palm Jumeirah would rarely ever think of moving to any other location in Dubai. Breathtaking sunset views with record-breaking numbers of "likes" on social media, beach clubs, waterparks, shopping and retail centres, fabulous fine dining, promenades, green parks, and jogging tracks—you can have it all there without needing to leave the Palm. There is always something to do and experience.

Residents of Emirates Hills appreciate the finer things in life, as the community sets the highest standards for an opulent lifestyle with top-notch amenities and an array of recreational facilities. The community is home to celebrities, politicians, and influential personalities.

Along with the aforementioned posh communities, there are many other new and established family-oriented communities in Dubai that offer beautiful properties with top-notch amenities, and they all come with different price tags, from affordable to luxurious, offering great value for money.

Now that you have got an understanding of the lifestyle property concept, it's time to start exploring what is right for you. Pick from one to three communities for the next weekend, and explore them.

One of my friends, who is a seasoned golfer, was exploring options of a home on a golf course. I've always wondered why golf is such a popular sport. "Because of its soothing effect," he told me. He had done his homework and shared several things to take into consideration before buying a golf course property.

One of the most important things when considering where to buy a property is to get a sense of the environment from people who actually live there. Besides exploring the community, he took it one step further and talked to the residents. "Do not hesitate, go talk to the neighbours in the area," he told me. "Ask your agent to connect you with people who bought properties here before you, preferably a few months back." These people would be your best source of information on how it feels to live in this community. They normally understand all the questions, because they probably had the same ones themselves. You will have a better idea from the insiders' perspective and make new friends. After you are done with your survey, you will have a much clearer picture. Don't forget to invite your neighbours to your housewarming party!

What he also discovered was that he was able to make good connections around this community while playing golf and enjoying the lifestyle. He met some influential people on the golf course, and his wife was able to connect with a few powerful clients for her accounting firm, while casually networking at the clubhouse. That kind of networking is a value-added feature of your community experience. Imagine, you no longer need to sign up for any special membership club or attend numerous events to network with the people of your preferred circles. You can do it from the comfort of your neighbourhood, in a relaxed, casual environment and naturally connect with like-minded people.

"It is better to see something once, than to hear about it a thousand times," states a popular proverb. Experiencing different lifestyles is a great way to feel and realise what is right for you. It might seem confusing, overwhelming, and time consuming to you; however, such confusions set when you go there with a busy mindset. It's important to take time and not rush through it.

If you skip experiencing lifestyles and hobbies and jump straight into window-shopping, you will be confused.

When you are in the right space with your mind at peace, you will feel it. To give you an example, one of my clients has recently found her "perfect home" after so many different, unsuccessful window-shopping attempts. To start with, we had a fair list of requirements in terms of the property specs and budget, so we started looking. Initially, she was convinced that she wanted a one- or two-bedroom apartment, so we first explored options according to that property type. As we were progressing, she realised that she was no longer considering apartments and wanted to explore townhouses, as she wanted "to have her own small yard." Fair enough, we switched to townhouses.

Her priority was ready-to-move-in property, as she wanted to move in right away. This left us with very few options, which were very challenging to consider with the budget she had in mind. Viewing after viewing, she was getting disappointed. As per her criteria, nothing impressed her. Until one day, when she walked into the sales office of the developer and absolutely fell in love with an off-plan apartment project by the sea. The ready three-bedroom townhouse on a tight budget and an off-plan apartment project by the sea that was twice her budget—these are two ends of the spectrum. However, the second option was exactly what she was looking for emotionally, while rationally her brain was telling her the complete opposite. I cannot stress enough how important it is to understand yourself and feel yourself and be able to identify which lifestyle is right for you at an early stage, before jumping into viewings. Otherwise, you risk wasting a lot of time and energy by looking in a completely opposite direction from where your happiness is.

This brings me to a point that I will be discussing in more detail in the next chapters—about our emotions and the role they play in our decision-making. However, for now, let's summarise the key points from this chapter.

First, you should decide the extent to which your property should cater to your lifestyle. For example, if you absolutely must play golf every morning, or the golf course or golf club is where most of your business meetings are held (I've seen buyers and sellers of this type), then the golf course property would probably be your best match. If you haven't yet discovered what your preferred lifestyle is, as you already know, the best exercise to help you to do so is to explore.

WHAT ARE YOU BUYING: PROPERTY OR LIFESTYLE?

On the other hand, if at this stage you are neutral to the add-ons of the lifestyle properties of this nature and will be fairly happy in a house that satisfies your basic and most important needs, then take it easy on this chapter; you can always revisit it later.

So think about planning your next weekend in a community that you have never been to before. For example, if you are living in an urban district like Downtown or Marina, go watch a polo game with a picnic basket or a golf game at one of the golf/polo clubs to feel the vibes of these so-called remote communities that are "too far away from the city." You will be surprised how you will feel about those "countryside" neighbourhoods. After a half day spent there, you'll more likely feel like you just came back from a vacation. And who knows, you might actually start considering them.

Pick a new community where you've never been or stayed before and book yourself and your family a "staycation," to experience this community. In fact, many people in Dubai rent houses year after year in different parts of Dubai to try new communities. You can do the same over a few weekends.

The idea is to get a feeling of your lifestyle vibes in the beginning of your search for a perfect home to use your time and money efficiently.

There is an obvious need to find something that excites you so that you and your family will live an exciting life in your new perfect home in Dubai. In the next chapter, you will learn how to actually find the exciting project that offers you your lifestyle.

HOW TO FIND A PROJECT THAT EXCITES YOU

Have you done or experienced anything exciting lately that is worth remembering?

Thinking of knowing what excites you is one thing, living the life full of excitement is another thing. Unfortunately, many people don't understand the difference between both these things. Some people actually know the difference; however, it's challenging for them to arrive from point A, by just knowing or imagining, to point B, which involves actually experiencing a life that's full of excitement.

How do you bring the excitement into your lifestyle? Simply by incorporating one by one all the things that matter to you. As mentioned in previous chapters, you start by exploring new experiences and places and then eventually finding yourself living in your happy home that provides you with all the features for your dream lifestyle. If you found out in your previous step that you actually are excited about waterfront living, this chapter will help you understand the methodology of picking the right waterfront or beachfront project in Dubai, according to your needs.

Let me tell you about one of my friends who had a really tough time choosing a project in Dubai as her holiday home investment. She got really excited about one specific project, and deep inside, she had a feeling that this property purchase should be exceptional and unique, that would make her feel good while living there, make her proud of the purchase, and also, she wanted to see value added in the future.

Keeping in mind "the best or nothing approach," she had budget and cash-flow limitations that she needed to match with the payment plan, and she absolutely didn't want to compromise on either of those. While looking for options, she discovered that there are many different beachfront options, offers, and incentives out there that perfectly matched her financial abilities. However, being already connected emotionally to one project that she liked, she imagined herself enjoying the lifestyle and the amenities in that particular beachfront residence. Hence, she could not look further, even though the terms of purchase were quite tough for her. In other words, she had found something that really excited her; in her case, it was the prime location, uniqueness, luxurious finish, layouts, and the overall concept of a unique product offering that would make her feel very special. Fortunately, she was able to get what she wanted for closing the deal, even though she had to compromise on the payment plan. However, finally, she was very happy, as she had managed to buy her exciting dream waterfront home.

HOW TO FIND A PROJECT THAT EXCITES YOU

This chapter alone, when read with great focus and attention, will give you clarity on the selection process of a project according to your criteria.

Life in Dubai is extremely busy, and we barely have time to waste it in traffic and long commutes. It's all about convenience here, and while searching for your perfect home, you should not compromise on convenience. In fact, this is what you should focus on to pick the community that will suit your lifestyle. Your perfect destination where you can live, stay, play, shop, dine, and work.

Close your eyes and imagine waking up every morning to the magic views of the waterfront or lush greenery, surrounding your house or community, having a smooth and easy commute to drop your kids at school on your way to work, without the hassle of having to waste your time in rush hour traffic. Then before coming home after work, you pass by your community retail centre, which is conveniently located just minutes away from your home, where your butcher has carefully chosen and prepared for you the best lamb cut, as he knows that on Thursday evenings, you traditionally cook a delicious barbeque dinner and invite your friends and neighbours. Here comes the next day, Friday, when, after breakfast, you let your kids play at the park nearby, where they meet other children, while you have time for yourself. This is what you really look for when you live in a community. A seamless experience full of joy and convenience with maximum comfort. Does it sound like a wonderful weekend in a dream home and dream community? Well, let's make this dream come true. Provided that you will carefully follow the methodology in this chapter, you will be able to draw a roadmap that will bring you the result that you are aiming for.

What is exciting about Dubai is that absolutely each and every community in this city has its own "thing," unlike in other cities in the world where the lifestyle experience gets exciting mostly near the downtown or only in a few communities surrounding the centre of the city. We are truly spoiled here, aren't we? However, the more choices we have, the tougher the decision-making process gets.

What I see, based on my experience of receiving inquiries from people from all over the world about buying a property in Dubai, is that the top four exciting things for international buyers in the hit parade are the following—proximity to and views of Burj Khalifa, demand for branded residencies (Armani, Bvlgari, Dorcherster, Versace), demand for properties with a private beach and/or yacht club, and a craving for "a peaceful, family-oriented community."

Now if I'd ask my friends and colleagues who have been living in Dubai for the past few years to share their views of exciting projects in Dubai, the results will be different. Imagine, families that have been living in Arabian Ranches for years. Do you think they care about the view of Burj Khalifa? Perhaps they certainly admire it, when taking their visiting guests and family members to the fountain show near Dubai Mall, but it's absolutely not a priority for their exciting lifestyle.

What do you need to take into consideration when you are searching for your exciting project/community in Dubai?

HOW TO FIND A PROJECT THAT EXCITES YOU

Start getting to know your preferences by asking yourself the following questions:

- What excites you?
- What can you absolutely not live without?
- What is the deal breaker for you when it comes to the community? Location/area, landmarks, features, or amenities?
- Do you want to live in a mature community, or would you be enthusiastic about choosing a developing community and see it growing and appreciating in value while you are living there?
- What do you want to do while you are at your community—enjoy dining, experience thrilling water sports, or jogging? What do your kids like to do—play in the park or walk your pets?
- Do you picture yourself living in the same community for the next five, ten, or more years?
- What about your family and friends who visit you from your home country? If they stay at your place, how easy it is for them to navigate the community by themselves, when you are busy all day at work? Are the shops close by? Can they go to the beach easily? Where is the closest mall?

Once you have your answers to these questions, you might already have a few projects in mind. Your memory might start recalling a specific area you visited a while ago where you liked the convenience and ease of getting in and out, or where you enjoyed that Friday ripe market setup and amazing family vibes environment of the community. Or maybe when you went for a brunch at the beach club, you just fell in love with that particular beach and then you remembered one of your friends telling you that actually there is a beachfront residence nearby that provides access to the same beach.

Typically, there are only one or two specific things about a place that catch your attention. Other features and amenities may still mean a lot to you, but it's those one or two features that really appeal to you. Those are actually the things that you need to define. Those would be decision-making drivers when it comes to choosing the project. These things just strike you, and the next thing you know—you have found it.

After a bit of brainstorming, I came up with the list of features that I would personally pay attention to. They are two different categories—things you can see and touch, and those that you can feel. I will let you go through the list of these keywords and come up with your own:

- Energy and ambience: peace and serenity or busy city vibes
- Exclusivity: gated or low density society
- Layouts and panoramic views
- Finishing quality and colour pallets
- Interior design and furniture
- Amenities, greenery, and landscaping
- Environment-conscious and sustainable
- Bespoke service/experience: how that experience of living in the branded residence makes you feel

After you get an idea from my list, do a simple exercise: try to remember when was the last time you really felt great about a

HOW TO FIND A PROJECT THAT EXCITES YOU

specific place or home, or even a hotel, and recall what exactly was in it for you—visual appeal, a feeling of comfort, sounds, colours, etc. Come up with your own list by brainstorming and keep it with all your other notes as you are reading this book.

Remember, finding out what really excites you is a journey. And the best way to find out is to explore. You will ask me, "Is this entire book about exploring?" Well, a major part of it is. My mission is to inspire you to live your life to the fullest, in the best property and community, according to your needs. In order to arrive at your dreams, there is only one simple exercise you need to do—ask yourself, experience, evaluate, and repeat. Let me inspire you by sharing the stories of other people, by telling you about their journey of finding that one project that was meant to be their perfect home.

My car got stuck in the sand as I was driving further down the beach. I got out of the car and quickly evaluated the situation; this was the first time I had got stuck in the sand, and I was in shock and felt helpless. I absolutely didn't know what to do in this kind of situation. After six years in Dubai, I still haven't become a pro in sand bashing.

I was not alone. I had a client whom I had brought to the project site to show the orientation of the buildings, the construction's progress, and that beautiful beach where we got stuck. Going above and beyond the average house-hunting process, my approach is to always get my clients to feel the project by making arrangements for them to experience the places. But this time, it looked like things were not going according to my plan.

In an attempt to salvage the situation, I told my client that it's going to be alright and suggested we leave the car and continue walking down the beach all the way to the water so that we could accomplish the mission. We reached the beach around sunset, when the sun was illuminating the skyline behind us, while creating beautiful shades of colours in the sky ahead of us. We went all the way to the water and stood there for a few minutes, enjoying the views of the skyline and horizon, listening to the sound of the waves, and inhaling fresh sea breeze. That was actually the moment of experiencing the place, the beach, and the community that I wanted to share. Needless to say, anyone who comes to this site falls in love with the vibes and the views. Despite getting stuck in the sand, we managed to do what we had set out to do, and that visit determined the choice of the project for my client. Still wondering how we got the car out? Well, we had to push it, and after a few attempts, I was able to get it out from the sand, so the story had a happy ending. ☺

For this methodology of experiencing new places to work, you have to think through it without rushing, have a brainstorm, and review it. Make a list of everything you are looking for in a home, big or small. If there are multiple people involved in the decision, have each person make their own list independently. Compare your list with those of the others and look for overlaps. Combine the common requirements into a new, narrower list.

For each requirement on the list, ask yourself, "If I found a house that was amazing in almost every other way, would I compromise on this requirement?" If so, it's a "good-to-have," not a top priority.

HOW TO FIND A PROJECT THAT EXCITES YOU

Once you have your list of top priorities, set clear parameters with your real estate agent, narrow your search, and avoid wasting time touring properties that would not be a good match.

I've met couples who disagreed on fundamental criteria like location and type of property, and, unfortunately, it takes a lot of time, effort, and energy for them to convince one another, which delays the search for their perfect home and complicates the process. Sometimes, different family members of different generations in a family have different things that excite them. So it's very important to discuss these things and work on it together in order to come to a conclusion.

To give you another example—a couple wanted to buy a property next to Deira, as they had spent over fifteen years in this area and didn't want to consider any other location. But their grown-up teenager daughter, for whom they were investing in the property in order to pass it to her, was considering other locations like Downtown, because of its different lifestyle and the urban city vibes that she liked. While investing in property and thinking of it as a multigenerational asset, you should carefully think of the changing environment and development of the city. So be clear on your priorities—whether it's your personal decision or a mutual one with your family members.

Life in Dubai is exhilarating, and you should be living it to the fullest, by choosing a suitable lifestyle and exciting community. There are many questions to ask yourself prior to searching for a community in Dubai. Ask yourself those questions, define and prioritise your criteria for the search, and know the most important item you must consider when looking for a home. Only you know what features are essential for you and your family. For many people, the first priority may be price, neighbourhood, or the number of bedrooms, or possibly some combination of the three. Someone else may list a backyard that can accommodate pets as their must-have feature before they will consider any other criteria. The point is that you must decide what aspects of a home are most important to you when you are in the market for a new home.

Go through the questions and prioritise your criteria; you could break this down very scientifically with an Excel spreadsheet, but a pen, piece of paper, and some honest conversation will also do. Also, make sure that you are fully aware of the things that you don't need—those features and amenities that are not necessary for you, but that can actually add to the cost of the house.

Now that you have completed the exercise, you should feel confident about the choice of community in Dubai, and this leads us to the next questions—how to actually find and choose the right property.

EVERY HOME BUYER'S DREAM

*If you haven't found it yet, keep looking.
Don't settle. As with all matter of the heart,
you'll know when you find it.*

—*Steve Jobs*

The perfect home in the perfect location at the perfect price—that's every home buyer's dream. And once you start your search, you realise almost immediately that it's more like a dream, and you might settle for less than perfection for the things that really matter to you.

The purchase of a property is a major decision in your life. So, how do you make the right choice?

By now, you have probably shortlisted at least a couple of communities to take a closer look at and are ready to jump directly to the right property analysis and selection. First of all, let's understand what the most common types of properties are that you will come across.

There are three major types of residential properties in each community in Dubai—apartments, townhouses, and villas—all based on different parameters and all having their pros and cons, which are determined individually for every home owner. It's important to understand the advantages and disadvantages that matter specifically to you before making a decision, and you'll also have to weigh your needs. You may want more room and more autonomy over your living space. Or you may prefer the convenience of apartment living, particularly in a complex that provides many services and features.

Apartment living has long been an attractive option for those who don't want to live in a full-scale house and deal with the maintenance of landscape, pool, etc. Living in an apartment complex usually brings access to a large array of amenities. This potentially includes things like a common room for hosting events, swimming pool, barbecue area, a gym, covered parking, and security systems. However, when it comes to space and storage, house owners almost always win. They have the advantages of such things as garages, attics, and more closet space. Additionally, due to the crowded nature of apartment buildings, the privacy afforded by apartment living is less than that of living in a stand-alone villa. You might overhear someone speaking in the apartment next to yours, or they might hear you, whereas when you live in a villa, you have more privacy.

This chapter will enable you to choose the right property among different options within the community.

I have worked with buyers who struggled to define what type of property they wanted, as they didn't a have clear picture of their dream home. Pushed by budget limitations and not knowing about flexible payment options, confused first-time home buyers were often ready to settle for less than they actually deserve—in other words, a smaller unit (apartment), while what they actually needed was a townhouse.

To better understand whether you are a villa or apartment kind of person, ask yourself the following questions:

- Summarise, in general, your previous housing experience and lessons learned, even if you were just renting a property before. Point out things that you didn't like and what you need to avoid when searching for your perfect home.
- How many separate bedrooms and bathrooms do you need?
- Do you need a garage or a parking space?
- Do you want a backyard, a balcony, or a terrace?
- Do you need an elevator? Do you have special needs in terms of accessibility?
- Is a separate entrance necessary?

Summarise the advantages and disadvantages of each property type for you by going through the table below.

Comparative table for apartments, villas, and townhouses

	Townhouse	Villa	Apartment
Affordability	The most affordable	The most expensive	More affordable than a villa
Backyard/Plot	Small	Large	n/a
Extra storage/ maid's room	Large	The largest	Smaller than for a townhouse or villa
Views	Limited	Better than views from townhouses	Could be exceptional/or no views at all, depending on height and floor plan
Parking	Typically 2 parking spots, and not much space for street parking for visitors	Typically 2 parking spots, and, in most cases, option for street parking for visitors	Number of allocated parking spots will depend on the size of the apartment. Typically would be smaller, compared to villas and townhouses
Maintenance fees	Lesser than for a villa	Higher than for a townhouse	Lesser than for a townhouse or villa
Service charges	Typically similar if we are comparing villas and townhouses in one community		Higher than in villas and townhouses
Amenities and facilities (pool and gym)	As per the community centre/ clubhouse, public access	Can be customised and built on the plot, provided that the size allows, private access	As per the building, public access

Once you have a better understanding of what kind of property type is most suitable for you, let's go through some tips on how to choose the unit within the building/community and how to pick the right one for you.

Do you want to have easy accessibility, to be quickly in and out from your house in the community?

- Yes -> then you should consider picking a building/unit close to the road that is next to the entrance/exit of the community.
- Doesn't matter -> all right, you have more options to choose from, since you are not limiting yourself to the units close to the community entrance/exit.

Do you want to have immediate access to the pool and clubhouse in the townhouses/villa community?

- Yes -> pick the unit within walking distance from the pool/community centre. Be prepared to pay extra for this, as normally the units that are located next to the parks, community centres, kids play area, and the pools are priced higher than the rest of the units in the community. If you decide to rent it at some point in the future, typically you can demand higher rent for it and it normally gets rented faster than other units.
- No -> great, you have an entire community to choose from, and if you are not bothered about walking a bit more or even driving, you can save a good amount of money by picking a unit that is not directly located close to the community's amenities.

Corner or middle unit of a townhouse?

- Corner unit -> if you need a more spacious layout, bigger plot, and more privacy, this will be costlier than the middle unit.
- Middle unit -> a nicely picked middle unit would also do well, provided that the amount of space is exactly the space that you need, and it matches your budget requirements.

Higher floor, lower floor, ground floor of the apartment?

- Higher floor -> if you are really looking for a nice view, a higher floor would do better. Be prepared to pay a higher price, though.
- Lower floor -> for those who would feel safer close to the ground and are not really fond of the high-floor views. Typically, low to middle floors are the most affordable units in the building.
- Ground floor -> in most of the cases, this combines an experience of living in an apartment and at the same time having a large outdoor terrace space, as if you have your own backyard in a townhouse.

When I first moved to Dubai, I rented an apartment on Sheikh Zayed Road, close to the Dubai World Trade Centre. I found a very nice property in a brand new building that was just being handed over.

You know how you sometimes have these viewings during your lunch break, when you don't really have much time? So you walk into the apartments, take a quick look, and you feel like all of them are exactly the same, while you don't notice the orientation of the unit. The real estate agent responsible for leasing showed me a few options, and I really liked two units. Unfortunately, the unit with a lot of sunlight was rented the same day, before I came back with a cheque. I was a bit disappointed, and as I really liked the building and didn't want to start my search all over again, I just picked the other unit that I saw. I didn't pay much attention to the fact that the unit overlooked the backyard, had no view, and there was very poor sunlight during the day. It turned out to be a very dark apartment. I realised that only after I moved in, after all the formalities were done and the cheques were cashed. Thankfully, it was just a leasing arrangement, not a purchase. Imagine if you purchase a unit like this in a rush. So do not make hasty decisions. Take time at the viewings, check things thoroughly, pay attention not only to the height of the floor but also to the views, orientation of the unit, and the amount of sunlight. Even though layouts may look the same, the orientation of the unit is a game changer.

In order to choose the right property, do not make any assumptions until you experience a site visit to an actual unit or a show home; then you know your preference for either an apartment, townhouse, or a villa. It is absolutely necessary, despite making a checklist, to make a site visit coupled with a thorough analysis of different kinds of housings.

Although it can be discouraging to look at place after place and just feel, well, nothing, but don't get discouraged. When you find it, you'll know, and all the house hunting will have been totally worth it.

Beside emotional attachment to your dream home, you have to be aware of the home's ability to be resold. Poor location, road noise, neighbourhood nuisances, and other factors greatly reduce the desirability of a property and will make it harder to sell. While it may be tempting to buy a lower-priced home that is discounted for these reasons, the same will be true when choosing to sell it.

Everyone is different. What works for your friend, family member, or colleague may not work for you. Have a defined goal, and if you don't or can't articulate it clearly, make sure you are working with the real estate agent who can help you do so. You'll be better off in the long run if you prioritise your needs to know exactly what you are looking for. Know how to pick the best unit in the project according to your needs and preferences.

Go to the site visit keeping in mind all the major steps and note down all the comments:

- Do a viewing with the checklist in hand and make sure to tick the applicable boxes and note down the missing features.
- Have a separate checklist for each property you visit.
- Compare, analyse, and shortlist the options that are the best match according to your criteria.

Since we now know the details on how to choose the right property, the next thing we will cover is knowing yourself as a buyer and why it is important to know this when you are looking for a house. What's important to know is not only your financials and a list with your priorities but also how emotional or logical you are in the decision-making process. It will help you to avoid common mistakes, choose the right property, and win the best deal on it.

THE PSYCHOLOGY OF BUYING A HOME

People do not buy goods and services.
They buy relations, stories, and magic.

—*Seth Godin*

This quote by Seth Godin describes how we make the most of our purchase decisions. We are not led by rationality alone when deciding about the purchase. But how do emotional and rational purchases differ from each other?

For many of us, decisions are impacted by rational as well as emotional motives. Whether a decision is made based on emotional or rational factors is highly individual and depends on the person making the decision, the product, or other circumstances. For example, I remember myself buying things that I didn't need, while feeling good emotionally. Good mood and good vibes, an attentive and friendly salesperson, a bit of free time on that day when you were actually just passing by that store, and voila—you didn't notice how you swiped your card at the cashier's register. And the other way around, I remember that I was not able to make a purchase decision for the things that I rationally needed, just because the emotional component, or a trigger, was missing.

By the end of this chapter, you will understand what role your emotions play in the decision-making process of buying a property and how to actually make them help you in this journey.

You'd buy a sweater on impulse, but when it comes to buying a property, it's all about calm deliberation, right? You might be surprised. I recently witnessed a story that completely changed my view.

A few months ago, one of my colleagues met her client at one of the malls in Dubai. The lady was here on vacation for the first time in Dubai. She was at the mall to shop for some clothes and gifts; however . . . she ended up leaving the mall after signing an order to purchase a one-bedroom apartment. Surprisingly, this lady didn't have any intention whatsoever of buying any property, neither in her home country nor in Dubai in the near future. So what happened? She got emotionally attached to the idea of having a property in Dubai as her holiday home since she was overwhelmingly impressed by her experience in Dubai. It was an absolutely emotional purchase, and not logical. Let's understand better what role emotions play in our decision-making process.

Emotional purchase
I have researched the topic and discovered that neuroscientists conducted a study which found that people who were

unable to generate emotions due to medical conditions had trouble making decisions. The criteria that impact our emotional purchase decisions are highly personal:

- Love/sentiment
- Envy
- Pride
- Entertainment
- Vanity

For emotional purchase decisions, it can be argued that the need does not necessarily have to be present in the first place. Rather, it is created by external sources. Thus, these purchase decisions are strongly based on impulses as well as recommendations. There is no long-term need or any urgent circumstance that leads to purchasing a product. Sometimes we do not look for information prior to the purchase and do not evaluate alternatives. The decision is purely based on an emotional input.

Rational purchase

Rational purchases are those purchases that are mainly based on objective criteria:

- Profit
- Security
- Caution
- Health

For these, rational factors outweigh emotional ones. We buy a house because we want to ensure we have a home to live in. Rational purchases are accompanied by extensive research and comparisons of different products and offers.

A home is a place where you'll create memories, and for some people, there is a strong sense of emotional attachment. It's no surprise that a decision like this comes with a lot of emotion. Buying a home is a big deal, and the decision-making process is even more complex than you may think.

We all know the logical questions to ask ourselves. Is it the right price? Is this the right location? What we may not realise is the element of psychology that is present when deciding to buy a home. After months of research and deliberation, the average home buyer is confident that they are about to make a completely rational buying decision; however, the opposite is often true. Educating yourself on the psychology behind buying a residential home and absorbing these hidden details will empower you to make a more informed decision.

We let our emotions blind us to cold facts about the market or the realities of ownership. Or we prioritise one set of emotional needs over others that are just as strong but may not be evident at first. And ignoring them can lead us to make bad financial decisions that can affect us for decades to come. Do you remember walking into the store, wandering around without an intention to buy any specific item, until the moment the salesperson approached you and made you feel special about something, and that feeling then triggered your interest and need to buy a specific item? I remember many cases like that, like buying a new Nespresso machine, while initially shopping just for capsules. My decision to buy was emotional, not logical.

I felt my way to a reason to buy. Being emotional while buying a house is a good thing when you have that feeling that it's your place from the moment you entered the door. On the other hand, you should be very cautious when you get extra excited and lose connection with your reasons and requirements that you outlined in previous chapters. This is when you should step back and get more analytical, rather than emotional.

For instance, people might focus on their desire for a house that's a certain size or style but ignore the fact that they want to spend as much time as possible with family. So they might buy a "perfect" house that requires them to make a long daily commute to work and keeps them away from home.

One of the biggest trade-offs is commuting. Many people move to live in a bigger house, but that bigger house is often further away from work—so that means more commuting, which tends to add stress and detract from overall happiness. If you're moving to a place far away from your friends, but it has nicer stuff, it's not always a great deal for your happiness.

At one point of time, when I was moving from one apartment to another, I was seriously considering picking a place next to the area where majority of my friends live. Proximity to the location where they live and where we normally get together was almost top priority criteria along with the budget in my list. When I asked myself what the emotional motivation behind the criteria of being close to my friends was for me, it was a sense of belonging to a community, to a group mindset, sharing the same lifestyle, getting together frequently with a shorter commute. I felt that I would be isolated if I moved further out, even though in Dubai it takes you pretty much fifteen-twenty minutes by a car to get anywhere. Finally, I picked a location without compromising on budget and commute, and found what is called the "golden mean."

Getting ahead of the subtle details that can influence our decisions is important, and asking the right questions at the right time will help. So what should you be aware of when you are on a mission to find your perfect home?

Emotions
Before any viewing, have your requirements set on non-negotiables, i.e., the right price, location, number of rooms, etc. Doing so will help keep emotions in check when you fall in love with a home that comes above the asking price or when it comes with two rooms and you were looking for four. If you are leaning towards a house because of its "feel good" factor, try to identify the emotion behind it. For instance, you can strongly feel something about that beautiful two-bedroom apartment, but you know it isn't perfect for your requirements, as you need four bedrooms plus a room for the maid and a spacious storage room. Try to capture and recognise what specifically made you feel so good about this place and recreate it in another home or add the criteria that you just discovered to your list for further reference.

Naivety
First-time home buyers need to understand that they are buying more than just a house. They are purchasing a lifestyle and this concept should remain top of their mind throughout the entire process. First-time home buyers' naivety has the potential

to lead them away from their original goals. Let me further explain my thesis that naivety is one of the biggest dangers in the process of home buying. There are a number of ways you can be naive and, quite frankly, taken advantage of. This is because there are many specific but diverse activities you will engage in before you successfully move to your new home.

These activities include:

1. Assessing where to buy your new property—the location
2. Assessing the physical condition of the property
3. Organising the finances
4. Negotiating the deal

Each of these four areas is a potentially tricky area on its own, but combine it with any of the other three areas, and it's easy to see how you can make costly mistakes through naivety.

The best approach to take is to ensure you receive good advice at every step of the way, so you have to engage the help of professionals.

For example, being very naive, some buyers will move to a neighbourhood on the wrong side of town, forgetting that they can easily buy a house at a more attractive price further out in the city, or they can fix up a house that needs renovation, but they can't change the location of the house.

Another example: sometimes, buyers may not believe that the price is an accurate assessment of the house's market value.

They submit very low offers and then get frustrated when their offers are consistently rejected. Furthermore, some buyers don't trust real estate agents and may even try to buy their home without an agent, which is generally an unwise choice. In Dubai, you will need the assistance of a professional and licensed real estate agent and the banker or mortgage broker. Ideally, your real estate agent will connect you with all the necessary parties in the deal.

Real estate agents invest a lot of their time and energy to source suitable options for you, so respect their efforts and time they invest in your home search. Be honest and always declare if you need more time to digest info and reevaluate your search criteria. Also, be careful with the advice given not only by the agents but also by your friends. No one knows better than you what kind of house you will be happy to live in, so listen to the advice, but make sure to do your own analysis. It's your responsibility and no one else's to find and select the perfect home for you, and there is no one to blame if you end up buying something that you were advised against.

Men's approach to buying a property
Interestingly, based on my observation, men and women have quite different ways of looking at the search process, decision-making process, and the buying process. Let's go through them one by one.

Parameter 1. Size
For men, the total size of the property is much more important than the layout itself. While women, as they go through the property, start imagining the decor and how the furniture

will be placed, based on the possibilities of the layout. Men, on the other hand, are ready to change the layout (if permitted so) for their own needs. For example, demolish or build walls, add features, etc. In general, men will prefer a larger apartment with almost any layout against small-scale housing with successful zoning, which is so attractive to women.

Parameter 2. Safety
For men, the expression "my house is my fortress" is extremely relevant, meaning that the house should be a calm place where they can relax after work, leaving all the problems outside. Men would typically equip the house with video surveillance, cameras, and other modern devices. In addition to security, men really value privacy. They will never choose a house that allows for a window-to-window format.

Parameter 3. Technical state
If the responsibility for interior design and the look and feel of the home is almost always taken care of by women, the technical state of a property is always the men's area of responsibility. Men pay almost no attention to the interior, believing that insignificant wall scratches can be easily fixed by repainting the walls; however, they do examine the flooring, pipes, plumbing, and electrical work very thoroughly.

Parameter 4. Minimum options
As opposed to women, men do not intend to study dozens or hundreds of proposals until they find the perfect one. They tend to make decisions quickly, as they aim for a result rather than a process. Most men need "just a good option." And for this purpose, it is enough for them to see two to five

properties. If they find that one of the options has met several important requirements, they stop searching, as they consider further research a waste of their time.

Parameter 5. Uniqueness
Men need everything exceptional, exclusive, ideally existing in a single or very limited edition so that they can tell their friends about that rare piece of marble that he has chosen himself from the factory in Italy and brought to this master bathroom in that unique full-floor apartment with an exceptional view of Burj Khalifa. I personally know buyers who went to Italy to select a unique shade of marble for their property renovation, so this kind of focus on uniqueness is not a joke. ☺

Women's approach to buying a property
Despite the fact that society is imbued with stereotypes about mysterious "female logic," unpredictable behaviour, and excessive emotions, in reality I must say those myths are not true when it comes to the process of women buying property. Converting myths into features, here's what I noticed.

Parameter 1. Intuition
The statement "Women fall in love through their ears" does not apply to real estate purchases. When choosing a property, they rely on their inner voice, not on the words of others. Women trust only their own impressions obtained during the viewings, by looking at 3D images, renderings, and layouts. While viewing potential properties in the secondary market, ladies walk dimensionally through the rooms and stand by the windows. At this time, they visually analyse whether this fits into the image of their "perfect house." And their intuition gives them an answer.

Parameter 2. Perfection
As opposed to the belief that women don't know what they want, it turns out that they know extremely well what they want. You ask me, but what if a woman went to the store for a beige coat and came back with a red handbag? Well, it doesn't mean that the lady didn't know what she wanted. When the perfect coat wasn't there, why would you let go the opportunity to get a flawless red handbag that was on your wishlist anyway? The conclusion is that the object of desire has to be perfect according to their requirements.

As already noted, when selecting a car, apartment, or any other thing, men are normally result-oriented and want to conclude the matter fast. While women are looking for a dream property until they are sure that they've seen everything and that the option they are choosing is the best. At the same time, women compare potential properties by a large number of criteria. They are concerned by the size of the kitchen and living room; the capacity of closets, cabinets, and other interior items; as well as the infrastructure of the community, proximity to schools, shops, etc. The search will end only when the entire puzzle is completed.

Parameter 3. Deliberation
Also, the female's principle of impulse purchases in most of the cases does not apply to real estate. When choosing properties, women carefully analyse all offers and then examine the best ones. The probability that women will sign the deal after visiting the first two-three properties is close to zero; they are just getting warmed up and enthusiastic at that point. Even after shortlisting a couple of suitable options, women will

continue to further explore for even greater perfection. On the contrary, men are ready to sign a contract of sale immediately if a particular property meets the basic criteria.

Parameter 4. Cost-conscious
Despite the fact that women easily spend money on themselves, spending money left and right does not apply to fundamental acquisitions, like a property purchase. Furthermore, ladies like to bargain a lot so as to allocate the savings for furnishings, interior design, and landscaping.

Parameter 5. Adapt and improve
Even if a woman wants a man to deal with the financing of the property, she has to choose a dream house herself, since the probability of a man "guessing" 100 per cent on all the features of her dream house is small. However, in the case of a gift or surprise purchase by a man, a woman will accept the man's choice and slowly incorporate interior design, decorations, and furniture to her taste.

These tips should help couples to consolidate their efforts in the home-buying process through a better understanding of the different approaches that ladies and gents have.

Now that you have hopefully recognised your behaviour patterns in some of the stories in this chapter, try to maintain a balance between being intuitively emotional and rational at the same time in order to make the best decision to find your perfect home. It won't work if you go to a viewing without setting your priorities in terms of technical characteristics, as you have to stick to certain criteria. However, it won't also work if you are just going to measure everything by logic, using facts and numbers, without giving yourself room to find your perfect home with your feelings too. Find your perfect balance for logic versus emotion.

Our emotions play an important role in our decision-making process. Nonetheless, we need rational triggers to satisfy our needs as well. Instead of just aiming for a purely rational or exclusively emotional strategy, a good mix of logic and emotions can be more beneficial.

- It's scientifically proven that a first-time home buyer's decision is greatly affected by emotions
- There needs to be a healthy balance between emotions and logic while making a decision
- For your emotions to help you find the perfect home, make sure to consider the points mentioned in this chapter

The next viewing you go to, make sure to feel and analyse your emotional connection with place, your reaction on presentation, etc., and then make a conclusion. However, do not forget that decision-making is a practical task. Therefore, you should incorporate pragmatism into your decision-making process.

DUBAI: HOLIDAY DESTINATION, INVESTMENT, OR HOME?

There's no place like home to enjoy your holidays, and it's even better when you're vacationing in Dubai and feel like you're at home.

Based on my observation, almost every other family or businessperson that has been frequently visiting Dubai for at least two or three years in a row for vacation or business considers having a holiday home here to save on the cost of hotel stays and also to feel like they are at home while being away from home. In addition to being a nice place that you can always come back to, your Dubai holiday home can also generate good returns that will allow you to not only cover the cost of the maintenance but also get very attractive returns on your investment.

With so much going on and so many people arriving, the short-term rental market has come of age at the right time. Holiday homes provide the necessary accommodation for a spectrum of budgets and in any location in Dubai. You can now rent a one or two-bedroom apartment for the price of a single hotel room. This means that you can travel with your family, make your own food, wash your clothes, and have enough space for everyone. Owners could either be investors looking to make money from their property or frequent travellers wanting to make a profit while being away on a holiday. By the end of this chapter, you will learn about the Dubai holiday homes concept and what's in it for you—whether you are already a resident in the UAE, a frequent visitor, or thinking of relocating here.

Having lived in Dubai for almost six years, I have witnessed a number of initiatives that the UAE government has launched in order to attract growing numbers of visitors, unlike any other country in the world. Dubai caters to visitors from all over the world by offering not only luxury hotels, first-class dining, and superb shopping malls but also family-friendly entertainment venues, theme parks, beaches, cultural activities, museums, and world-famous tourist attractions, including the Burj Khalifa and Dubai Mall.

Ever since a legal framework for holiday homes was introduced in 2016, the industry has been booming, with more and more homes coming on the market each day. From solo travellers to large families, there is something for everyone. While having a great time in the sun by the sea and enjoying your vacation in Dubai, the idea of having a holiday home here will naturally flow into your mind during the very first days of your vacation. If you come to Dubai with your family and rent a holiday home you can easily calculate the amount of money that the landlord of the property is receiving for your stay. Or let's say you are staying with your big family at the hotel and booked

DUBAI: HOLIDAY DESTINATION, INVESTMENT, OR HOME?

two rooms, as you can't all fit in one room. Then calculate your expenses for stay, extras for laundry, meals, etc. Now let's compare your expenses of renting a holiday home and living in a hotel. Provided you are comparing hotels and residences in the same location and more or less of the same quality. I bet you will spend much more on a hotel stay. Now ask yourself—why would you pay for a hotel when you can buy your own property and actually be that landlord who receives the money from people like yourself, who prefer to have a cost-effective stay, without compromising on space and quality of the accommodation. After that "aha moment," your holiday home search takes another round—now you are looking not to rent but to buy your own holiday home in Dubai.

While the decision of getting a holiday home might be emotional, you should clearly know the reason why you are considering owning a holiday apartment in Dubai—is it for lifestyle or for investment, or is it a mix of both?

Depending on certain reasons, there are typically two scenarios in your decision-making process. If your holiday home is to be a lifestyle property for yourself and your family to spend time during vacations in Dubai and you are not planning to rent it out, then the selection process will pretty much depend on your preferences, without taking into consideration how rentable it will be. Lifestyle properties within branded or serviced residences are exceptional investment options for UAE residents, as well as global investors looking for a second home to grow their asset portfolio. If this holiday home property is purely for regular rental income, then it's a numbers game on returns that you can maximise, without your personal preferences and emotions attached to the selection of the property. In case it's both, then the decision-making process is a bit more complex, and I suggest that you run through the points below.

What should you know before buying a holiday home?

1. Ensure you purchase in a prime location
When selecting holiday home investment properties, choose a prime location near all the "must-haves," such as restaurants, cafes, shopping centres, and tourists hotspots. Proximity to the beach and a sea view makes a big difference when it comes to success with a holiday letting.

2. Choose the size of the unit
Since many holiday apartments are built for short-term rentals, they have smaller layouts. While studios may yield a higher rental return on the purchase price and are perfect for investment, a one-bedroom unit gives you an option to move in yourself if you ever decide it's time for a change of lifestyle. So, ask yourself how you see yourself using this holiday home a few years from now. Will it be just for investment or for personal use?

3. Choose a professional management team
Ensure that the management of the complex you are considering has a strong track record in apartment complex management as well as a comprehensive understanding of the highly competitive holiday accommodation market. An experienced and professional management team could make the difference between an empty and occupied apartment.

4. Do your calculations
Holiday rentals are usually much higher than those for normal properties and increase even more in peak season. This may make the initial sums for holiday properties look great. However, you will need to allow for longer vacancy periods and fluctuating occupancy levels from season to season.

Also, remember that every week you stay in your holiday property is a week less of rental income you will receive. And the times you would usually like to stay in your apartment will be the times that most other tourists would want to stay there too.

Short-term rental of holiday homes as an investment
Dubai offers significantly higher property rental return compared to London, New York, Hong Kong, and Singapore. The increasing number of tourists and also regional and global corporates who bring their executives on a short- or long-term basis to Dubai created an opportunity to look at serviced holiday homes as a lucrative income-generating asset. Consumers today are more sophisticated; they are looking to experience the best of both worlds—the luxury and amenities of a five-star hotel in the comfort and privacy of a home. This demand represents an opportunity to tap into the market of hotel apartments and serviced branded residences, where you get a "turnkey solution." In other words, everything from the dining table and chairs to the bed linen is taken care of.

So what does a buyer or tenant look for in a branded or serviced residence? It's a different kind of offering that elevates their living experience. Such residential properties not only incorporate great design but also offer the benefits of lifestyle concierge services, tailored packages, and other privileges. The prime location of these properties is another critical factor that guarantees higher occupancy in these branded, serviced residences.

Other factors that make serviced apartments an attractive choice for investors are ease of sale owing to short-term guests as compared to traditionally rented properties that require an advance notice to the tenant. The properties are maintained excellently, to ensure that high standards are in line with most brand guidelines.

Your "turnkey" holiday home property appeals to short-term tenants, end users, and investors. While a property that is rented on an annual contract can only be bought by investors, a short-term property is vacant to transfer and can be considered by both investors and end users. That's why majority of the short-term apartments can be offered simultaneously for sale at any time. This gives you, as a property owner, a stronger negotiating position because you are earning a regular income.

What if you have already invested in a property that is not branded or furnished and you still want to rent on short term and have peace of mind that the property is being managed? Likely, there are companies in Dubai that will take care of your property by providing turnkey furnishing solutions, interior design services, marketing and customer service, adhering to the highest standards of comfort and convenience for the guests, while making sure it is cost-effective to the property.

Supported by continuous government initiatives to strengthen Dubai tourism, the real estate sector, and the city's ranking as

DUBAI: HOLIDAY DESTINATION, INVESTMENT, OR HOME?

a top international hub, the holiday home market in Dubai is set to grow significantly over the next few years and provide lucrative investment opportunities.

Through my experience, I helped buyers to source and acquire holiday homes in Dubai that they would use purely for themselves without renting them out during their absence. It's understandable, as not everyone will let out their exclusive penthouse with designer furniture or their customised beachfront villas to tourists on short terms. Even though it will make sense from the investment point of view, because the rental income can cover property management expenses, the fact is that, emotionally, people don't want to let out their carefully chosen and furnished property. I've been managing properties that have been completely revamped with a new design concept, that come with meticulously customised landscaping and gardens, and that are holiday homes properties where the owners spend just a couple of weeks a year. So holiday homes properties are chosen, managed, and operated on an individual basis. As long as you know what you want, there is always an opportunity to match your requirements with a wide array of property management services.

If you don't live in Dubai and want to get a holiday home here, whether it's for investment or for yourself, my advice would be to work only with a reputable agency and specifically with an experienced real estate investment broker with a proven track record in acquiring and successfully managing large portfolio or properties. Do your research and pick a professional that handles all aspects of property investment from A to Z. If you live in Dubai, things get a bit easier in terms of due diligence on the best property investment, as you can physically go and see the sites. However, you are much better represented when you are backed up by the opinion of an industry professional, so make sure you also get an experienced real estate broker on your side.

Having a holiday home in Dubai and letting it for a short term can be a great way to make money and generate passive income. Financially speaking, renting properties in the short-term market can be a great way to maximise your return on investment, especially with the booming Dubai tourism market.

To get an idea of what you can make through short-term rentals, do your online research by browsing property portals and checking the rates for one-bedroom apartments and studios in areas with the highest demand, like Downtown, Dubai Marina, and Palm Jumeirah. Pick one area after another and study each of them carefully in order to understand what you can potentially make by letting your holiday home for short terms.

HOW DO YOU FINANCE YOUR PROPERTY?

Your cash versus mortgage? Everywhere you look, you hear that it's bad to carry debt. So naturally, you will think that buying a home with cash is a smart choice. Is it really? Or is it always a smart choice?

There are many different ways of financing your property in Dubai. In most cases, your decision will be tied up closely to the type of property that you are choosing. For example, if you are selecting an off-plan property, you have an option to go with the payment plan from the developer. In case you are going for a ready property, in most cases, you would consider a mortgage financing with the bank. There are also cases when you are considering an off-plan property, but you can still benefit from the payment plan during construction and then you have an option to mortgage it on completion. And another case is when you are going for a ready property with a payment plan. In this chapter, you will learn how to choose the financing method that suits you the best.

When it comes to property purchase, the main question that buyers ask themselves is—whose funds should they use? There is a certain category of buyers who would prefer to use cash to pay for the property, and in most cases, they would prefer to pay it upfront so they don't have to pay interest and they don't owe the bank any money. On the other hand, there are people who prefer to use somebody else's money in order to finance their property, while they would invest their money in either their business or other asset classes.

The truth is that there is no right or wrong approach. It all depends on each individual's situation and the cash flows they want to maintain. For example, recently, I came across a very nice couple who have been living in Dubai for three years, and they decided to buy a house here. They really liked one of the upcoming off-plan townhouse projects and were very excited that the developer offered an extended payment plan, as they were not really keen on paying the bank the interest rate. However, after they carefully calculated the cost of renting for three years and paying the instalments for their property at the same time, they realised that this would stretch them a lot financially for the next three years. As a result, they had to change focus from the first project that they liked, and we started to look for mortgage options with ready-to-move-in properties, as it was the only solution to finance their new home.

HOW DO YOU FINANCE YOUR PROPERTY?

Now, let's take a closer look at four different scenarios of property financing and look at the pros and cons of each.

1. Off-plan property with payment plan

Many developers are offering off-plan properties with an initial down payment, which typically would be anywhere from 5-10 per cent in majority of the cases, and the balance would be spread out over the period of construction (typically three years). In some cases, there is even an option to have an extended payment plan, also called post-handover payment plan, where the remaining balance of instalments is paid over a certain period of time after construction is completed.

This kind of arrangement would be beneficial for those buyers who don't mind buying properties during construction, as they don't need to move in right away, and they are used to the concept of investing in early stages of the project. Those buyers typically have a steady cash flow, allowing them to plan their instalments according to the payment plan.

2. Ready property with full cash payment or bank financing

For some first-time homeowners, it is very important to buy a ready property, which they first want to see physically and inspect, as they don't really appreciate the concept of buying a property "just on paper." Secondly, they would need to move to the ready property from their current rental property as soon as possible. This dramatically increases the urgency of moving to their own property and finally not paying rent, especially after calculating the cost paid during the years of living in Dubai. I recently came across a statement saying, "Congratulations! Ten years in Dubai and still haven't bought a house? You actually gifted your landlord one." That's the painful reality for many families that have been living in Dubai for over a decade. For buyers who are rushing to switch from renting to owning before the commencement of their next rental term, there are typically two scenarios—paying with their own capital or getting a bank financing.

While I am not going to get into the details of bank financing, interest rates, and terms of down payment for mortgages (as they vary for UAE residents and nonresidents, and terms change from bank to bank), I'd rather touch again on the concept of choosing between putting 100 per cent of your money and using a bank's money.

In general, for those buyers who would like to remain liquid or use their cash for other investments, the preferred scenario would be going through a mortgage. The rationale behind it is the comparatively low interest rates for mortgage and the opportunity to make more profit on the money invested, to cover up the cost of mortgage.

However, there is also a category of buyers that does not want to invest their money widely and at the same time prefer not to lose money on interest rate payments either. They would go with the full cash payment option to have peace of mind from having no financial liabilities with the bank.

3. Off-plan property with a payment plan and bank financing option at completion

Luckily for those who like the off-plan options with their payment plan, there is an option to consider getting bank

HOW DO YOU FINANCE YOUR PROPERTY?

financing upon handover of their property, in case, if some time down the line, they would need to get bank leverage to have a longer repayment period.

This option represents an excellent opportunity to spread a down payment into instalments during the construction process, so you don't have to have 20 per cent down payment at the moment of signing the deal. All you need is 5-10 per cent down payment; the remaining 15-25 per cent can be covered during construction and then you can mortgage the balance on completion of construction.

4. Ready property with the payment plan
This, by far, remains the most popular option among a majority of the buyers on the current market, as it allows to move in straightaway into the property by paying just an initial down payment up to 25 per cent (it varies from project to project) and have the instalments payments of the balance spread over a few years after moving into your own property.

The variety of financing and payment plan options represents an excellent opportunity to buy a property without having 100 per cent cash in hand. As you can see, the dream of having your own property is not a dream anymore; rather it becomes a reality sooner or later, once you go through your finances and do the necessary financial planning.

As the financing is always the deal breaker, I strongly advise you to start off the entire process of financial planning by consulting first with the banker or mortgage broker in order to run the preapproval for the financing amount. Unfortunately, eliminating this step could cause major time and effort loss for all participants of the process—buyers, sellers, and their respective agents. When the buyers jump straight to the viewings, their disappointment comes after they fall in love with the property, which they can't afford, as it turns out the mortgage preapproval amount is not covering the closing price.

Now that you have gotten an insight into the different payment schemes, you have to understand your cash flows and match it with the payment terms applicable to the type of property you are considering.

Knowing how to structure and plan the financing of your first property is very crucial to your financial success and prosperity in the future. Having a clear idea about your options and possibilities to finance the property is important before you sign any document. Let's summarise the major scenarios of financing the purchase of your property:

1. Off-plan property with your own cash payments on the payment plan.
2. Ready property with full cash payment or bank financing.
3. Off-plan property with payment plan and bank financing option at the completion.
4. Ready property with a payment plan.

If you are considering buying a ready property with mortgage, your next step would be to get mortgage preapproval from the bank to what amount you can borrow. After getting your mortgage preapproval for a certain amount, you will be

HOW DO YOU FINANCE YOUR PROPERTY?

able to narrow down the options within the range of your eligibility.

If you are considering getting an off-plan property or a ready property with a payment plan, then you would need to carefully study the payment plans of all the options that you have checked already, and see which one works better with your cash flows. There could be room for negotiation on the payment plan; however, make sure that you are being realistic about your possibilities so that you will be able to pay according to the plan without stretching your finances, taking into consideration all other expenses and liabilities you have.

Now that we covered all the major tips on how to find, choose, and finance the property in the previous chapters, let's go over the common mistakes to avoid during this process in the next chapter, to make sure that you are 100 per cent ready to find your perfect home!

COMMON MISTAKES TO AVOID

*Always try to learn from other people's mistakes,
not your own—it's much cheaper that way.*

—Donald Trump

Buying a new house is a huge step, so it is important that you make your decision very carefully. Small mistakes and ignorance can cost you a lot. If you are not careful, buying a new home can become profoundly exhausting and scary, instead of exciting. It is a massive financial investment, so make sure that you avoid any mistakes that can harm or halt your investment.

In this chapter, you will learn about the most common errors that can prove to be very costly and shatter your dreams of buying a new home, so do go through this chapter carefully so that you can learn how to calculate and address all the risks involved in the home-buying process.

What normally stops us from doing or pursuing things in life? I am sure everyone will come up with their own list of reasons;

however, they would all come down to two major points—risk and fear. I hear stories from my friends and my clients who have had a bad experience buying properties. The most common risk that they actually faced is a delay on the delivery of the project and handover of their property, which resulted in major negative impact on their wealth.

While the risk of the delay is something that a buyer cannot mitigate unless choosing a ready property, there are other risks and mistakes that can be prevented by the buyer, so let's look at them one by one.

1. Being influenced by market news
Don't be influenced by "the market" more than by your own needs. The property market moves in cycles, and there are times when they suit buyers; at other times, it is a sellers' market, when prices are booming. However, waiting for the "right time" or for the prices to go down is gambling with your family's future. If you know your budget, have your finances organised, and think about your current and future needs, then you should rarely let short-term market conditions influence what will be a long-term lifestyle decision.

2. Not knowing your budget
Having a very clear budget in your mind is important. Work out your budget by listing all the monthly expenses, including the rent, cost of commuting, loan and credit card payments, insurances, utility bills, etc. Subtract this amount from the take-home pay and you will know the exact sum of money you can afford to spend on your monthly repayments of mortgage or payment plan.

If you don't have a budget, you will waste your time and the time of all the people involved in the viewings of those properties that you cannot afford. Furthermore, you may end up getting emotional without having a clear number in mind and invest in a place that you cannot afford. This can have a huge negative impact on your financial well-being in the future.

3. Differentiate between price and value
We all know that to make money on a property, you should ideally close it with a price that is below the market when signing the deal. However, it doesn't mean you must buy cheaply. You make your money by buying the *right* property, not a *cheap* property. Price is what you pay; value is what you get.

You can always buy cheap properties in secondary locations, but to be stuck with your capital in a secondary property that is not sellable or rentable—that is not a good idea. Do not make **your buying decision based purely on price; always think about the value for money that you are getting.**

4. Not considering added costs
Buying a house is not as simple as it looks, as there are so many things that you have to consider. It is not just a simple act of moving from rent payments to paying the mortgage. There is the closing cost, insurance, home owner's association fee, etc. Most home buyers have all the major costs in mind, but they fail to consider other costs such as maintenance costs. It is possible that when all the costs are included, the house is over budget. That is why it is important to sum up all the possible costs before making any decision. You can get an estimate of the entire cost by asking about average maintenance, cost of

insurance, and so forth. Add them to the monthly mortgage or payment plan installment to know exactly how much the house will cost you.

5. Going unrepresented
You probably have good research and analysis skills to gather important knowledge about the property market, the area you are interested in, and the overall home-buying process. What you probably don't have, however, is perspective and representation.

The sellers have an agent protecting them, looking after their interests, and advising them on the best asking and closing prices. Why do most home buyers go solo then? You might have done extensive research and house hunting, but this is likely to be your largest purchase ever. And your emotions and lack of proper information may cloud some of your decisions.

That's why it's important to have equal protection on your side, like the seller has. The seller's agent will always negotiate on a higher closing price, and you, as the buyer, do not want that. Your real estate agent has access to market analytics that you do not always have. The data from recent transactions in the area where you are looking to buy a house is key when it comes to the final closing price negotiation. That's why it's critical to engage a professional buyer's agent to represent your interests in the entire process from viewings to negotiation.

You wouldn't go to court without a lawyer on your side—would you?

6. The "sick and tired" or "desperation" purchase
You've been doing viewings for a few months already but haven't found your perfect home. The family is upset, while the agents are attacking you; you have submitted few offers, but they were not accepted. **You are sick and tired of this entire process and just want to get it over as soon as possible.**

One huge mistake that first-time home buyers make is to buy a property in desperation. They will finalise on something reasonable rather than something that really suits their needs because they're sick of the emotional rollercoaster of the process of home buying. **This is a decision that you may regret for a long time.**

Rather than buying because you've had enough, stop your home-search process for a while, and take a break. Also, work with only one agent, a truly professional and passionate one, who will understand your needs and priorities and will only inform you of suitable options to save your time and effort.

7. Thinking this list is exhaustive
It's not. There are so many other issues to consider. But if you already can cope with this list of the most common mistakes, then you are ready for a much more efficient home-buying process.

Sometimes you just want something so bad that you make an emotional decision without actually forecasting long-term implications and calculating risks and hoping these things will work out by themselves in the future. As discussed in previous chapters, emotional decisions can have a serious impact on your financial situation in the future, especially when you are buying a property that you cannot easily afford on impulse. One of my friends booked her property with a personal loan that she utilised for her mortgage down payment. Central banks and mortgage lenders don't allow personal loans to be used for down payment. Using a personal loan defeats the purpose of the down payment contribution, since the payment is supposed to show that you're investing some of your money.

On top of that "double commitment," I must say that she bought her property when the market prices were on the rise. Now, a few years later, once she finally finished the payments towards her down payment loan, the market prices went significantly down. Now, the worth of her property is almost equal to the amount of the down payment that she borrowed. Just imagine buying an overpriced property with a double financing commitment. She has lost so much money paying interest on her personal loan and the mortgage. Not to mention the stress and financial pressure that she has been through over the years to be able to meet these commitments.

Before we end the chapter, let's recall once again the most typical mistakes that first-time home buyers tend to make:

- Being influenced by the market
- Not having a clear budget
- Making decisions based on the price rather than considering the value
- Not considering added costs

- Not engaging a professional real estate agent and mortgage or insurance broker
- Making a rushed or desperate decision

Go through the above-mentioned mistakes and analyse your previous big purchases. Did you make any of these mistakes? Congratulations, if you did not! However, if you did, it could be a great lesson learned for you, and now you can avoid making a mistake with a larger purchase.

Now that you are familiar with all the typical mistakes that can be very costly and shatter your dreams of buying a new home, you can take preventative measures by doing your research more thoughtfully, engaging experts to support you in this journey, and dig into areas that you need to focus on. Let your first-time home-buying process be a joyful and exciting journey.

CONCLUSION

My dear reader, I am delighted that you have read my book. By now, you have probably already realised that there is never a right or perfectly scheduled time to do anything in life. Once that time passes, we regret that we haven't done that particular thing that we wanted to do before.

It applies to all things in life—whether accepting that job offer, dating that girl or that guy, trying that experience, or making a buying or investment decision. Generally, in life, the earlier we make a decision, the better it is. If we make a good decision, we succeed; if the decision leads us to failure—well, we can learn from this failure and have more time to turn the failure into a learning experience, and then succeed.

When you are buying a home in Dubai, you are in fact buying into a lifestyle, so there is an obvious need to find something that excites you so that you and your family will live an exhilarating life in your new, perfect home in Dubai. You can always review the step-by-step advice I have given you to identify your lifestyle preferences. Remember that unless you choose a property that fulfils your lifestyle, you won't feel excited about your home.

The perfect home in the perfect location at the perfect price—that is every home buyer's dream. While nothing is perfect, we always strive to match our expectations to the maximum. In the race for perfection, focus on the things that really matter to you the most.

Be aware of your emotions, which play an important role in your decision-making process. Being emotional while buying a house is a good thing, on the one hand, when you have that feeling that it's your place from the moment you entered the door. On the other hand, you should be very cautious when you get extra excited and lose connection with your reasons and requirements that you outlined in the previous chapters. This is when you should step back and be more logical, rather than emotional.

If you google the most stressful events in people's lives and buying and selling a home, buying a home is very high on the list of stressors. This guide was designed to provide you with all the necessary information to prepare you factually and psychologically to walk through this journey with the least amount of stress, fear, and uncertainty. I wrote this book with a purpose—to give you full support to accomplish the important mission of finding your perfect home, where the dreams of your family will come true.

I have helped many first-time home buyers to achieve their dream in finding the right home that is as close to perfection

CONCLUSION

as they imagined it in their dreams, and my mission is to help as many people as I can to do the same. Should you need further guidance, advice, and motivation in this process, please reach out to me through the contact details mentioned in the "About the Author" section.

Generally, the process of buying a property is like climbing a mountain. But once you get to the top of it, you will experience that unparalleled feeling of accomplishment after you finalise the purchase of your first property. That feeling just cannot be compared to anything else. I sincerely wish you good luck with your home search and hope you soon reach the top of your mountain. Now that you have all the tools for finding your perfect home, and feel empowered, go out there and use them for the benefit of your future.

ABOUT THE AUTHOR

By now you already know about Anastasia's bio from the first chapter "My Dubai Story", but just in case you need a quick summary, here are few facts:

Anastasia is a licensed real estate expert in Dubai. Throughout her career and before shifting to residential real estate sales, Anastasia held positions within business development and marketing across investment, financial services, and management consulting industries. She has an MBA in International Business Management from a US-based university.

Her passion for lifestyle properties combined with her empathy and desire to help people define and find their dream homes led her to create this book.

Go to www.AnastasiaDorokhina.com to get further inspired about getting your perfect home in Dubai and get in touch with Anastasia to discuss how she can help you with that.

www.ingramcontent.com/pod-product-compliance
Lightning Source LLC
Chambersburg PA
CBHW021156080526
44588CB00008B/372